STARLIGHT & MOONSHINE

Poetry of the Supernatural

WILLIAM SHAKESPEARE
STARLIGHT & MOONSHINE
Poetry of the Supernatural

ILLUSTRATIONS BY

JANE BRESKIN ZALBEN

Foreword by Werner Gundersheimer
Director, The Folger Shakespeare Library

ORCHARD BOOKS
A DIVISION OF FRANKLIN WATTS

New York • London

*With love to my mother who makes magic
for my own two elves, and to the memory of
my father whose integrity and generosity will
remain a part of them forever.*

Library of Congress Cataloging-in-Publication Data
Shakespeare, William, 1564–1616. | Starlight & moonshine.
Summary: Selections of Shakespeare's verse with supernatural themes or subjects,
taken from "Macbeth," "A Midsummer Night's Dream," and other plays.
1. Supernatural—Juvenile poetry. 2. Children's poetry, English.
3. Songs, English—Texts. [1. Supernatural—Poetry. 2. English poetry]
I. Zalben, Jane Breskin, ill. II. Title. III. Title: Starlight and Moonshine.
PR2842 1987 821'.3 87-5789
ISBN 0-531-08328-4 (lib. bdg.) | ISBN 0-531-05728-3

CONTENTS

Tell me where is Fancy bred,
Or in the heart, or in the head?
How begot, how nourished?

The Merchant of Venice: Act III, scene II

FOREWORD

We think of William Shakespeare as a writer for all time, but he was first and foremost a man of the Renaissance. For all its scientific advances, and despite such breakthroughs as printing, the mariner's compass and the telescope, Shakespeare's world harbored an immense variety of imaginary, supernatural creatures.

Popular folklore offered a universe of invisible beings— goblins, elves, fairies and sprites. Some, like witches, embodied the dark, sinister side of the human soul. Others were benign, and reflected the positive enchantments of white magic, a subject that fascinated the adventurous.

For Shakespeare, the uses of enchantment were various and complex. In *The Tempest* and *A Midsummer Night's Dream*, we seem to enter fairy-tale realms, where in return for agreeing to suspend our tendencies to question and doubt, we are given brand new worlds of fantasy and beauty. The witches in *Macbeth* and the ghost in *Hamlet* intrude on a more human space and evoke deeper, more elemental responses. Shakespeare, immersed as he was in both the popular and the high culture of his time, fully appreciated the appeal of these beings and beliefs for his audience.

While superstition lives on today in all sorts of forms and few are entirely free of it, our imaginative horizons are in danger of becoming narrowed in scope even as they have expanded in space. A fictional alien from another planet cannot take the place of Ariel, nor will computer-created comedy supplant that of Bottom. Books like this one serve to renew our delight in fantasy and imagination. With her delightful illustrations of some of Shakespeare's most enchanting texts, Jane Breskin Zalben helps us to visualize that innocent, vanished world conjured up by his poetry of the supernatural.

Werner Gundersheimer
Director, The Folger Shakespeare Library

Ariel's Song

Where the bee sucks, there suck I;
In a cowslip's bell I lie;
There I couch when owls do cry:
On the bat's back I do fly,
After summer merrily.
Merrily, merrily, shall I live now,
Under the blossom that hangs on the bough!

The Tempest: Act V, scene I

Queen Mab

O then, I see, Queen Mab hath been with you.
She is the fairies' midwife, and she comes
In shape no bigger than an agate stone
On the forefinger of an alderman;
Drawn with a team of little atomies
Athwart men's noses as they lie asleep:
Her wagon spokes made of long spinner's legs:
The cover, of the wings of grasshoppers;
Her traces, of the smallest spider's web;
Her collars, of the moonshine's watery beams;

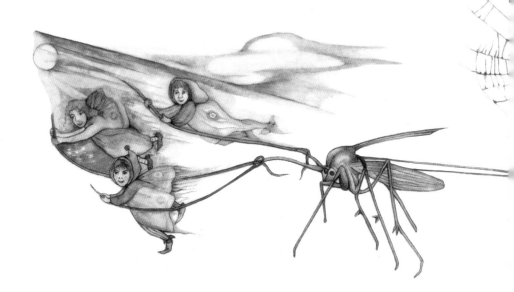

Her whip, of cricket's bone, the lash, of film;
Her wagoner, a small gray-coated gnat,
Not half so big as a round little worm,
Pricked from the lazy finger of a maid;
Her chariot is an empty hazelnut,
Made by a joiner squirrel, or old grub,
Time out of mind the fairies' coachmakers.
And in this state she gallops, night by night,
Through lovers' brains, and then they dream of love.

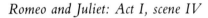

Romeo and Juliet: Act I, scene IV

Fairy Dance

Come unto these yellow sands,
  And then take hands:
Curtsied when you have, and kiss'd,—
  The wild waves whist,—
Foot it featly here and there;
And, sweet sprites, the burthen bear.
  Hark, hark!

The Tempest: Act I, scene II

Full Fathom Five

Full fathom five thy father lies;
   Of his bones are coral made;
Those are pearls that were his eyes:
   Nothing of him that doth fade,
But doth suffer a sea-change
Into something rich and strange.
Sea-nymphs hourly ring his knell.

The Tempest: Act I, scene II

Fairy Favors

Over hill, over dale,
Thorough bush, thorough brier,
Over park, over pale,
Thorough flood, thorough fire,
I do wander everywhere,
Swifter than the moon's sphere;
And I serve the fairy queen,
To dew her orbs upon the green:
The cowslips tall her pensioners be;
In their gold coats spots you see;
Those be rubies, fairy favors,
In their freckles live their savors:
I must go seek some dewdrops here,
And hang a pearl in every cowslip's ear.

A Midsummer Night's Dream: Act II, scene I

Titania's Request

Be kind and courteous to this gentleman;
Hop in his walks and gambol in his eyes;
Feed him with apricocks and dewberries,
With purple grapes, green figs, and mulberries;
The honey-bags steal from the humble-bees,
And for night-tapers crop their waxen thighs
And light them at the fiery glow-worm's eyes,
To have my love to bed and to arise;
And pluck the wings from painted butterflies
To fan the moonbeams from his sleeping eyes:
Nod to him, elves, and do him courtesies.

A Midsummer Night's Dream: Act III, scene I

Lullaby for Titania

Come, now a roundel and a fairy song;
Then, for the third part of a minute, hence;
Some to kill cankers in the musk-rose buds;
Some war with rere-mice for their leathern wings,
To make my small elves coats; and some keep back
The clamorous owl, that nightly hoots and wonders
At our quaint spirits. Sing me now asleep;
Then to your offices, and let me rest

You spotted snakes with double tongue,
Thorny hedgehogs, be not seen;
Newts and blind-worms, do no wrong,
Come not near our fairy queen.

Philomel, with melody
Sing in our sweet lullaby;
Lulla, lulla, lullaby, lulla, lulla, lullaby:
Never harm,
Nor spell, nor charm,
Come our lovely lady nigh;
So, good night, with lullaby.

A Midsummer Night's Dream: Act II, scene II

Love Song

Come, sit thee down upon this flowery bed,
  While I thy amiable cheeks do coy,
And stick musk-roses in thy sleek smooth head,
  And kiss thy fair large ears, my gentle joy.

A Midsummer Night's Dream: Act IV, scene I

Puck's Song

I am that merry wanderer of the night.
I jest to Oberon, and make him smile,
When I a fat and bean-fed horse beguile,
Neighing in likeness of a filly foal:
And sometime lurk I in a gossip's bowl,
In very likeness of a roasted crab;
And when she drinks, against her lips I bob
And on her withered dewlap pour the ale.
The wisest aunt, telling the saddest tale,
Sometime for three-foot stool mistaketh me;
Then slip I from her bum, down topples she,
And 'tailor' cries, and falls into a cough;
And then the whole quire hold their hips and laugh;
And waxen in their mirth, and neeze, and swear
A merrier hour was never wasted there.

A Midsummer Night's Dream: Act II, scene I

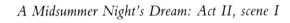

Remedy

On the ground
Sleep sound:
I'll apply
To your eye,
Gentle lover, remedy.
When thou wak'st,
Thou tak'st
True delight
In the sight
Of thy former lady's eye:
And the country proverb known,
That every man should take his own,
In your waking shall be shown:
    Jack shall have Jill;
    Nought shall go ill;
The man shall have his mare again,
And all shall be well.

A Midsummer Night's Dream: Act III, scene II

Fairy Visitation

Through the house give glimmering light
By the dead and drowsy fire;
Every elf and fairy sprite
Hop as light as bird from brier;
And this ditty after me
Sing and dance it trippingly.

First, rehearse your song by rote,
To each word a warbling note:
Hand in hand, with fairy grace,
Will we sing, and bless this place.

With this field-dew consecrate,
Every fairy take his gait,
And each several chamber bless,
Through this palace, with sweet peace;
And the owner of it blest,
Ever shall in safety rest.
      Trip away;
      Make no stay;
Meet me all by break of day.

A Midsummer Night's Dream: Act V, scene I

Gathering of Witches

When shall we three meet again
In thunder, lightning, or in rain?
When the hurlyburly's done,
When the battle's lost and won.
That will be ere the set of sun.
Where the place?
Upon the heath.
There to meet with Macbeth.
I come, Graymalkin!
Paddock calls:—anon!
Fair is foul, and foul is fair:
Hover through the fog and filthy air.

Macbeth: Act I, scene I

The Witches' Cauldron

Round about the cauldron go;
In the poison'd entrails throw.
Toad, that under cold stone
Days and nights hast thirty-one
Swelter'd venom sleeping got,
Boil thou first i' the charmed pot.

Double, double toil and trouble;
Fire burn and cauldron bubble.

Fillet of a fenny snake,
In the cauldron boil and bake;
Eye of newt, and toe of frog,
Wool of bat, and tongue of dog,
Adder's fork, and blind-worm's sting,
Lizard's leg, and howlet's wing,
For a charm of powerful trouble,
Like a hell-broth boil and bubble.

Double, double toil and trouble;
Fire burn and cauldron bubble.

Scale of dragon, tooth of wolf,
Witches' mummy, maw and gulf
Of the ravin'd salt-sea shark,
Root of hemlock digg'd i' the dark,
Add thereto a tiger's chaudron,
For the ingredients of our cauldron

Double, double toil and trouble;
Fire burn and cauldron bubble.

Cool it with a baboon's blood,
Then the charm is firm and good.

Macbeth: Act IV, scene I

Hecate's Song

I am for the air; this night I'll spend
Unto a dismal and a fatal end:
Great business must be wrought ere noon:
Upon the corner of the moon
There hangs a vaporous drop profound;
I'll catch it ere it come to ground:
And that distill'd by magic sleights
Shall raise such artificial sprites
As by the strength of their illusion
Shall draw him on to his confusion:
He shall spurn fate, scorn death, and bear
His hopes 'bove wisdom, grace, and fear;
And you all know security
Is mortals' chiefest enemy.

Macbeth: Act III, scene V

Spell

The weird sisters, hand in hand,
Posters of the sea and land,
Thus do go about, about:
Thrice to thine, and thrice to mine,
And thrice again, to make up nine.
Peace! the charm's wound up.

Macbeth: Act I, scene III

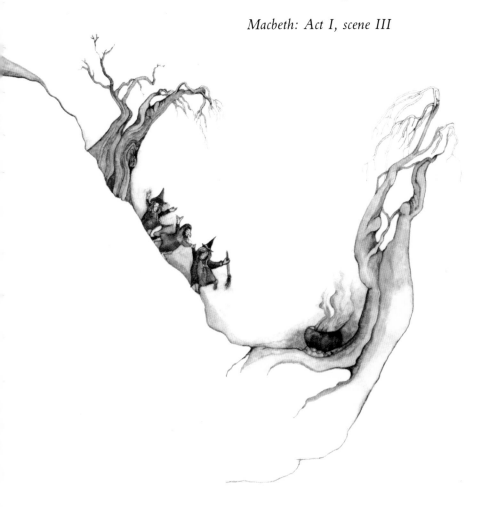

Night

Now the hungry lion roars,
    And the wolf behowls the moon;
Whilst the heavy ploughman snores,
    All with weary task fordone.
Now the wasted brands do glow,
    Whilst the screech-owl, screeching loud,
Puts the wretch that lies in woe
    In remembrance of a shroud.
Now it is the time of night
    That the graves, all gaping wide,
Every one lets forth his sprite,
    In the church-way paths to glide:
And we fairies, that do run
    By the triple Hecate's team,
From the presence of the sun,
    Following darkness like a dream,
Now are frolic; not a mouse
Shall disturb this hallow'd house:
I am sent with broom before,
To sweep the dust behind the door.

A Midsummer Night's Dream: Act V, scene I

Prospero's Spell

Ye elves of hills, brooks, standing lakes, and groves,
And ye that on the sands with printless foot
Do chase the ebbing Neptune, and do fly him
When he comes back; you demi-puppets that
By moonshine do the green sour ringlets make,
Whereof the ewe not bites; and you whose pastime
Is to make midnight mushrumps, that rejoice
To hear the solemn curfew: by whose aid
(Weak masters though ye be) I have bedimm'd
The noontide sun, call'd forth the mutinous winds,
And 'twixt the green sea and the azur'd vault
Set roaring war; to the dread rattling thunder
Have I given fire, and rifted Jove's stout oak
With his own bolt; the strong-bas'd promontory
Have I made shake, and by the spurs pluck'd up
The pine and cedar. Graves at my command
Have wak'd their sleepers, op'd, and let 'em forth
By my so potent art.

The Tempest: Act V, scene I

Prospero's Curse

Go, charge my goblins that they grind their joints
With dry convulsions, shorten up their sinews
With aged cramps, and more pinch-spotted make them
Than pard or cat o'mountain.

The Tempest: Act IV, scene I

Fairy Song

Fairies, black, gray, green, and white.
You moonshine revelers, and shades of night,
You orphan heirs of fixed destiny,
Attend your office and your quality.
Crier Hobgoblin, make the fairy Oyes.

Elves, list your names; silence, you airy toys!
Cricket, to Windsor chimneys shalt thou leap;
Where fires thou find'st unrak'd and hearths unswept,
There pinch the maids as blue as bilberry.

The Merry Wives of Windsor: Act V, scene V

Fairy March

Up and down, up and down;
I will lead them up and down:
I am fear'd in field and town;
Goblin, lead them up and down.

A Midsummer Night's Dream: Act III, scene II

Falstaff in Fairyland

Pinch him, fairies, mutually;
Pinch him for his villainy;
Pinch him, and burn him, and turn him about,
Till candles and starlight and moonshine be out.

The Merry Wives of Windsor: Act V, scene V

Ceres and Iris

Hail, many-colored messenger, that ne'er
Dost disobey the wife of Jupiter;
Who with thy saffron wings upon my flow'rs
Diffusest honey-drops, refreshing show'rs,
And with each end of thy blue bow dost crown
My bosky acres and my unshrubb'd down,
Rich scarf to my proud earth—why hath thy Queen
Summon'd me hither, to this short-grass'd green?

A contract of true love to celebrate,
And some donation freely to estate
On the bless'd lovers.

The Tempest: Act IV, scene I

Marriage Blessing

Honor, riches, marriage blessing,
Long continuance, and increasing,
Hourly joys be still upon you!
Juno sings her blessings on you.
Earth's increase, foison plenty,
Barns and garners never empty;
Vines with clust'ring bunches growing,
Plants with goodly burthen bowing;
Spring come to you at the farthest
In the very end of harvest!
Scarcity and want shall shun you,
Ceres' blessing so is on you.

You nymphs, call'd Naiades, of the wandring brooks,
With your sedg'd crowns and ever-harmless looks,
Leave your crisp channels, and on this green land
Answer your summons, Juno does command.
Come, temperate nymphs, and help to celebrate
A contract of true love, be not too late.
You sunburn'd sicklemen, of August weary,
Come hither from the furrow and be merry.
Make holiday; your rye-straw hats put on,
And these fresh nymphs encounter every one
In country footing.

The Tempest: Act IV, scene I

Caliban's Music

Be not afeard, the isle is full of noises,
Sounds, and sweet airs, that give delight and hurt not.
Sometimes a thousand twangling instruments
Will hum about mine ears; and sometimes voices,
That if I then had wak'd after long sleep,
Will make me sleep again, and then in dreaming,
The clouds methought would open, and show riches
Ready to drop upon me, that when I wak'd
I cried to dream again.

The Tempest: Act III, scene II

Our Revels Now Are Ended

Our revels now are ended. These our actors
(As I foretold you) were all spirits, and
Are melted into air, into thin air,
And like the baseless fabric of this vision,
The cloud-capp'd tow'rs, the gorgeous palaces,
The solemn temples, the great globe itself,
Yea, all which it inherit, shall dissolve,
And like this insubstantial pageant faded
Leave not a rack behind. We are such stuff
As dreams are made on, and our little life
Is rounded with a sleep.

The Tempest: Act IV, scene I

AFTERWORD

William Shakespeare's portrayals of the supernatural kingdom of fairies, elves, witches, ghosts and spirits are unique in English literature. Possessed of a rich treasury of knowledge of the most varied kind, he gives us, in his poems and plays, a rich picture of life in the Elizabethan era. He seems to have had not only a deep familiarity with the manners and customs of the time, but also an intimate acquaintance with the folklore of bygone days.

In Shakespeare's day, fairies were much in fashion, and so it is not surprising that he gave these delightful creatures prominent roles in many of his works. References to fairies in both earlier and contemporary literature set forth the characteristics of the various kinds of fairies, and Shakespeare was careful to describe them accurately. Some fairies, for instance, like Mab or Ariel, are extremely tiny and dainty. Others, called "day fairies," as in *The Merry Wives of Windsor*, are the size of children.

Puck is a different kind of creature—he is the jester of the fairy world, rough, faun-faced, and full of tricks. He is either related to or is, by another name, actually Robin Good-fellow, a hobgoblin. The Icelandic *puki* evokes the same kind of being, as do the Cornish *pixey* and the Devonshire *piskey*; all are derived from the same word.

Titania and others in her retinue refer to humans as "mortals"—an indication that she and her fellows were *not* mortal. They also refer to themselves as spirits, ghosts or shadows. Fairies in general were thought to be protective of humans; they were mischievous but not evil, and this is the role they are given in Shakespeare's poems and plays.

More sinister supernatural creatures were the witches who appear in several of Shakespeare's plays. It is not surprising that Shakespeare made use of these characters in his work, for belief in witchcraft was still widespread in the sixteenth and seventeenth centuries. The witches in *Macbeth* were based on commonly known figures from Scottish folklore, with perhaps some references as well to Scandinavian *norns* or fates. Hecate is, of course, from a more ancient tradition, being an avatar of Diana, but because it was common in the Renaissance to combine the ancient and the contemporary, this should not be considered an anachronism. More goddesses from classical literature appear in other plays.

In Shakespeare's time, the belief in ghosts was especially prevalent. These supernatural spirits were said to dress and look exactly as they had before death, but to maintain stubborn silence until they were addressed. Thus Hamlet asks Horatio, "Did you not speak to it?" Ghosts cannot bear the light, so disappear at cockscrow in his plays.

Caliban is a particularly intriguing member of the company of Shakespeare's supernatural creations. "A freckled whelp hagborn, not honoured with a human shape," he was a sort of sea-monster, with certain magical-seeming abilities. The name Caliban seems to be derived from the word "cannibal," and many of Caliban's characteristics are similar to traits ascribed to natives of the recently discovered New World of the Americas, in accounts written by over-imaginative sailors and by explorers of the time.

Shakespeare's portraits of supernatural creatures are drawn from his own deep familiarity with the traditional folklore and beliefs of his time, and they reveal to us a fascinating aspect of this many-sided genius. They also contain some of his most beautiful and imaginative songs and poetry.

A.K.B.

INDEX OF FIRST LINES

Printed and bound in Japan
Book design by Jane Breskin Zalben
The text and display type of this book is set in Bembo.
The illustrations are done in pencil, ooo brush
and watercolor, reproduced in halftone.
1 3 5 7 9 10 8 6 4 2